To family and friends past and present
with whom I have shared my life.

To my editor, Wendy Murray,
for her steadfast guidance, support, and encouragement.

— D. L. H.

Text copyright © 2004 by David L. Harrison
Illustrations copyright © 2004 by Boyds Mills Press

Published by Wordsong
Boyds Mills Press, Inc.
A Highlights Company
815 Church Street
Honesdale, Pennsylvania 18431
Printed in China
Visit our Web site at www.boydsmillspress.com

Publisher Cataloging-in-Publication Data (U.S.)

Harrison, David.
    Connecting dots : poems of my journey / by David L. Harrison ;
illustrations by Kelley Cunningham Cousineau. —1st ed.
[64] p. : ill. ; cm.
Summary: Poems that explore the poet's life from childhood through adolescence,
marriage, life as a writer, to being a grandfather and more.
ISBN 1-59078-260-7
1. Children's poetry. I. Cousineau, Kelley Cunningham. II. Title.
811.54 dc22   2004

First edition, 2004
The text of this book is set in 12-point Goudy.

10 9 8 7 6 5 4 3 2 1

Introduction

OF ALL THE EVERYDAY EVENTS IN OUR LIVES— being with friends, going to school, taking trips with family — why do some memories remain beacon bright while others fade away? The ones we'll remember may not even seem important at the time. A few we wish we *could* forget! But we can't. They have become part of us. It's a mystery. Maybe we remember times that somehow move us, touch our hearts, shape our ideas about life.

Poets pay particular attention to such memories, turning them this way and that, creating poems like tiny crystals reflecting our past. Put enough poems together, a surprising thing happens: a portrait emerges, like connecting dots until a picture appears.

The poems in this book are "dots" of my life — from early times to now. When you read them, they turn into a picture of me. I hope my poems inspire you to think about memorable experiences in your own life. I hope you'll write poems to connect some dots of your own.

David L. Harrison
Springfield, Missouri

CONTENTS

Section One: Ages 4–13
Before This Minute

Section Two: Ages 14–19
Around The Corner

Section Three: Over 20
In Your Wildest Dreams

Acknowledgments

Finding an inspection tag in new blue jeans makes us feel better about our jeans. Some eagle-eyed inspector at the factory held this garment up to the light, twisted it this way and that, checking for pulled threads. In that spirit, we chose an inspector for this book.

Veronica Pelliteri was twelve when she held these poems up to the light of her experiences and told me what she saw. Veronica helped so much that we set out to find other inspectors. This book has far fewer pulled threads because my inspectors would not allow them.

At PS 86 in the Bronx, Bela Kletnick, Arlene Rosen, Renny Santos, Robert Pape, and Susan Livingston shared poems with their kids from third grade through sixth and sent me their comments. In Decatur, Georgia, Marcia Poole and Marcia Pauly told me what their sixth- and seventh-grade students saw. Julie Strickland, elementary teacher and librarian in Moultrie, Georgia, shared her valuable thoughts and insights. And so did educator Ruth Nathan in California and poet Rebecca Kai Dotlich in Indiana. Worthy inspectors were discovered in Jennifer Harrison and her fourth-graders in Beaverton, Oregon; Nancy Raider and her fifth- grade kids in Springfield, Missouri; and Kathy Holderith and her third-graders in Littleton, Colorado. Teachers/writers Catherine (Cat) Doty who taught poetry in New York City and Laura Robb from Winchester, Virginia, stretched my thinking further about what middle school students respond to.

To my wife Sandy, always my Number One reader, and as eagle-eyed as they come, my gratitude. And to Wendy Murray, my editor and co-conspirator throughout this project, thanks for listening at the right times and leading when I needed it.

Section One
Ages 4–13

Before This Minute

Everything we experience before this minute becomes part of who we are now. That's why I started this book with poems about early experiences. Pushing my dog off the back step when I was little earned me the scar on my right thumb. It also taught me to be gentler. From a bear scare in the woods, I learned that even parents can be frightened, but they still protect you.

Do you ever feel sad, left out, not good enough? I think everyone does now and then. Remember being afraid of a bully? I do. Ever wonder about the other gender? Who doesn't! Poems in this first section talk about things like that. Perhaps you've had the same experiences in your own way.

I'm four. An elderly woman gives us Jigs, her English bulldog. Jigs teaches me that for every action there is a reaction.

Jigs

Jigs stands on the shady step,
feet planted,
ears bent,
red tongue dripping.

I need inside.
"Move, Jigs!"
I push him hard.

Panting,
wheezing,
gurgling deep,
he doesn't move.

I shove his shoulder.
"Move!" I say.

Pug nose wrinkling,
wet mouth opens,
snaps.

"Jigs!"

He jumps off,
waddles toward
quieter shade.

I stare in shock
at what he's done,
feel pain beginning
like fear.

Holding my thumb,
I run in,
screaming
disbelief.

I'm five. Our family has moved to Ajo, Arizona. In the backyard that backs up to ours, two neighbors have just returned from hunting in the mountains.

Mountain Lion

Hunters drag the lion
off the truck,
take turns posing,
holding its head.

Hands and knives
peel off the pelt
like a sweater tugged
over tight places,

Spread the pelt
for more pictures,
ignoring the carcass
drawing flies,
drying pink in the sun.

Watching, I wish
I'd seen that lion
high in the mountains,
walking in the sun.

I'm six. *We've lived in Ajo for a year when Granny Harrison comes by bus from Missouri. When she visits us, we eat hot Mexican food and laugh a lot. I don't know when I'll see her again.*

Goodbye Picture

The day Granny left,
we stood by the cactus
for a goodbye picture.

Daddy said, "Careful
you don't get stuck,"
but you know Granny.
Those cactus needles
burned like matches.

"Boy that hurt!"
she said in her letter.

"Glad we got loose,"
I said in mine.
    But not really —
now she's gone.

I'm seven. When you're a kid in a small town, you hear all the rumors. News moves fast, especially if it's bad.

End of the Walk

Rumors pull us
down the walk
to the place kids
aren't supposed to go,
to the bar
where they say
a man got killed last night

To see a stain
they say is there,
by the door,
where two guys fought.

I go to see
but not too close.
The air smells damp,
dangerous.
There's a stain there —
            dark —
            like blood —
or it could be dirt.

I wonder what
men think about,
men who think
they have to fight,
falling on a sidewalk
late at night.

I hope it's dirt.
I know I want to go.

I'm eight. My parents and I are camping at Whitehorse Lake in the White Mountains of Arizona. For the first time I learn that they can be afraid, too.

. . . .

Away from Camp

This morning bears came near camp,
woke us slapping steel bins,
grunting,
sniffing for food.

Dad listened outside the tent.
"It's okay," he said.
"They'll smell our scent,
won't come here."

After breakfast we took a trail
away from the bins
to look for deer.

A mile from camp
something noisy
crashed off suddenly
through the trees.

"Was that a bear?"

Dad stopped,
gripped my shoulder.
We turned around,
walked fast,
me looking back.

"Are we scared?"

"No," he said, hand on mine,
"Just a deer."

I'm eight. We move back home to Missouri in the winter and rent a small cottage on a horse farm. The weather seems bitter after the heat of Arizona.

Welcome to Missouri

Cold surrounds my warm spot.
Rolling over
is like touching snow.
I think of snow angels.

With extra clothes
piled on the bed,
I think of chalk outlines.
"This is where we found
the frozen body."

I miss my friends.
I hate this house,
the coal stove
with its belly full
of cold ashes.

Dad says soon
we'll find something better.

A prisoner inside
my own outline,
I wait for morning.

I'm eight. I started third grade in Arizona. My new school, just outside of Springfield, Missouri, is very different. It's hard being the new kid at Oak Grove Elementary School.

. . . .

Looking Away

What did you do
in school today?

I saw a boy
looking at me.
I waved,
he looked away.

His friends ran up,
yelling, laughing.
I laughed, too,
they looked away.

I answered wrong
in class today.
The boy laughed,
I looked away.

I'm twelve. The year I start seventh grade we leave Oak Grove and move into Springfield. Jarrett Junior High School feels big. I feel small.

Jarrett Junior High School

Kids here hit the hall
while the bell's still ringing.
Voices ricochet off walls,
the floor thunders.

Lockers open, bang shut,
groups form, block the fountain,
kids fly through
like guided missiles
pointed at their next class.

Lost, I slow down,
look for my room.
My body is a clock ticking.

Wrong room,
I turn back.
 "Watch it!"
Someone shoves me,
the bell rings.

Rooms suck in students,
leave the floor
like gray ice
when skaters are gone.
The empty hall falls silent.

My heart thuds
loud as my own late footsteps.

I'm twelve. Getting turned around in a new school is bad enough. Coming into class late is even worse. Some teachers give you a break. Some don't.

Price of Admission

I find my room
a minute after the bell.
The teacher keeps talking,
"Get out your books,"
frowns, points to the back wall,
the only empty table left.

Long walk to sit alone,
embarrassed by my failure.
She's not finished with me yet.
"Someone," she says,
"go join him at that table."

No one moves.
Who wants to choose
to sit beside the loser?
I shrink in the silence.
A chair scrapes.
A boy I've never seen before
plops his books by mine.

He writes a note:
"She gets real crabby when you're late."
I nod thanks.
In junior high, lots can happen
in a minute.

I'm twelve. Back at Oak Grove Elementary School guys played softball. I'm good at that. In town, they play basketball.

Hoop Lesson

The ball bounces down the court —
pa pa pa pa — shoes squeak,
guys grunt, dribble fancy
through their legs, pass
behind their backs.

Some days girls join the crowd,
yell for friends, guys wait
to play the winners, check
their watches, "Shoot! Shoot!"

I don't go there anymore
since the day they pulled
me onto the court. Someone
shoved the ball at me, "Play
guard," he said. "Bring it down."

How would I know what a
guard does? Basketball at Oak
Grove was one hoop on a dirt
yard, three guys laughing,
shooting a game of H-O-R-S-E.

"You gotta dribble!"
I tried, stumbled.
"Shoot!"
I passed.
"I'm open!"
I shot, missed.

They can shove their basketball.
I don't go there anymore.

I'm twelve. I stick with guys doing guy things. What girls do is a mystery. Sometimes they look at us and laugh. What's so funny? Boys don't have a clue.

Mysterious Birds

Girls whispering
in math class,

Passing
notes marked
with cutesy eyes,

Snickering
behind their hands,

Laughing
in the cafeteria,

Clustering
on the playground
like flocks of noisy
bright birds —

Don't they ever get tired
of all their racket?
Looking at us?
Making faces?

Whatever it is
that's so darned funny,
I'm beginning
to want to know.

I'm twelve. *I'm learning that some kids have it rough. I'm lucky. Maybe learning that is part of growing up.*

· ·

Paul

Paul's strong from cutting wood —
the family business.
He's not tall but his arms
have cords like a man's.

Broke his teeth in a fight.
Won, of course,
but now he never smiles.

He has no father since the night
his brothers had enough —
enough yelling, beatings, crying —
picked up firewood,
drove him off.

I look at Paul
and wonder why
I'm me instead of him.

Sometimes I watch my dad
laughing with my mother,
look at them,
        think of Paul,
try to understand.

__I'm thirteen.__ I've had a few trombone lessons, but now they put me in a band. I'm not ready.

No Way But Up

They put me down here
where beginners go,
end of the line —
thirteenth chair.

Practice scales
up the row
make me feel like quitting.

I frown at the music.
The notes look tangled
like strings of tadpoles
tied by their tails.

The baton taps,
jabs the air,
the band roars.

Trying to watch,
pump, blow,
follow notes
at the same time,
don't see the baton
stop.

In the sudden silence
I blurt out
two

     sour

        pitiful

           notes.

Heads swivel
like owls after
the same mouse.
The boy in first chair
looks at me and smirks.

I scowl his way.
Just you wait, I promise myself.
One of these days,
just you wait!

I sit up straight,
raise my horn,
ready for the baton.

Just

     you

        wait.

I'm thirteen. *Suddenly we're talking about girls. I know some kids who have gone on dates. We have more questions than answers.*

Some Things You Don't See Coming

Something happened over summer —
girls are looking different now.
Hard to say exactly how,
but other guys have noticed, too.
Seems like all we ever do
is sneak looks at girls.

Makeup maybe?
Clothes?
Perfume?
How they walk across the room?
Can't explain, I only know
(haven't told another soul)
I think I'm liking girls.

I'm thirteen. Joanne caught me off guard. Now I've got to learn how to skate before tomorrow night.

Mr. Smooth

Dumb Me, Chapter One

(Joanne)

"You like to skate?"

"You know how, don't you?"

"Our church is having
a skating party. Want to go?"

"Well sure, with me."

(Me)

"Uh-huh."

"Sure."

"With you?"

"Well sure."

Dumb Me, Chapter Two

I've never tried to skate before.
I've got one day to learn.
Why oh why did I say yes?
Trying to be Mr. Smooth I guess.
I should have told her no instead.
I'll probably fall and break my neck.
Either way,
I'm dead.

The Quiet Ones

Yesterday after school
Bobby tripped Wayne,
cussed him out.

Wayne got up,
started for the bus.
Bobby laughed,
pushed him.

Wayne stopped,
turned around.
Bobby dared him,
called him a coward,
shoved him harder.

Guys were shouting,
"Hit him! Hit him!"
Bobby sneered.

Wayne hit him
pop pop pop
too fast for Bobby to duck.

Bobby stared down
at the blood on his shirt.
Wayne climbed onto the bus.

Who knew Wayne
could hit like that?
Bobby didn't.

Today Wayne is quiet,
same as always.
Bobby doesn't know
what to do.

I'm thirteen. *Many of my friends from Oak Grove Elementary are now going to Jarrett Junior High School, too. But unless we're in the same classes, it's hard to keep in touch. Jarrett's a big place.*

Hey

At lunch today I see Billy.
"Hey," we say.
"How's it going?"
We don't stop to say more.
Can't think of anything.

From third grade on
we were best friends,
sleeping over
at each other's house.

Rode horses,
teased his sister . . .
I think of the night
we laughed so hard
he fell out of bed.

Now he's in homeroom 106.
I'm in 107.
And all we can say,
when we meet at lunch is,
"Hey, how's it going?"

Section Two
Ages 14–19

Around the Corner

I'M OLDER THAN YOU ARE SO I KNOW what's coming next, or at least what came next for me. I questioned why some kids were so popular. I thought about the way I looked. My friends and I wondered what our teachers were really like — what they did after school.

We started flirting more. Before long we were dating. I remember the excitement of learning how to drive and the awful shock when a friend died in a car wreck. Music and sports became important to me. I got my first job. And, I fell in love. Don't snicker. It could happen to you.

I'm fourteen. I look at the popular kids in school and wonder what they have that I don't. Some of them act so stupid. If you have to act stupid to be a leader, forget it.

How Do You Figure?

Jim makes me sick
acting like an idiot.
What do those guys
see in him?

If Jim says "Duh,"
they all say "Duh."
The dumber the better,
if it comes from him.

For a while they all said,
"Ain't it a jiggle?"
Now it's "Howdy Slim!"
Makes no sense,
but they say it and snicker,
grinning at Jim.

Today
he buttoned his shirt wrong.
Tomorrow
they'll do it, too.

I don't get it.
I want to be Jim,
but not if I have to be
like him.

__I'm fourteen.__ In junior high school, some guys like to act tough. Don's no actor. He's the real thing.

· ·

DON

He moves like royalty down the hall,
eyes flickering left, right,

Lion prowling for the kill,

Fighter headed
for the ring,

Don.

Don't let him look you
straight in the eye,
you don't want Don
to see you.

Yesterday he picked me out,
hit my shoulder
Bam!
like that.
Knocked me into a locker door,
hurt so bad I could hardly breathe.

Today guys ask me
how it feels
to take a hit from Don.
I look them straight in the eye,
whisper,
"You don't want to know."

I'm fourteen. One thing I'm learning for sure. The only thing worse than messing up is messing up in front of guys you know.

From the Back Row

Tonight our band performed at school,
on risers in the cafeteria,
music folders on black stands,
our first gig,
professional.

Trombone solo —
I stood tall,
pushed back my chair,
played flawlessly,
acknowledged applause,
nonchalantly took my seat.

Fell off backward,
trombone and all,
feet over head off the top riser,
somersaulted through the air,
crash-landed behind the band.

Applause and cheers when I reappeared,
climbed the risers
carrying my chair.

I wish I'd broken both legs.
A little sympathy
would help me a lot
tomorrow.

I'm fourteen. My first formal dance involves a corsage for my date, a boutonniere for me. Nights like this you remember your whole life. You'll see.

On the Tennis Court Under the Stars

The band begins its first tune,
paper lanterns tied on strings,
tables flickering candlelight.
Everything's different
on the tennis court under stars.

We all know we're here to dance
but who'll go first?
I feel the way I get
before a game.

Mary looks pretty.
Do I tell her that?
This isn't school,
it's a starry night.
My mouth is numb
like after the dentist
you can't talk.

Eyes closed, she sways to herself,
doesn't see the couples dancing.
It's now or never.
"Want to dance?"
Maybe she won't.
She smiles, says, "I'd love to."

I lift her hand like thin china,
touch her back low in the middle
the way I learned
at Walker's School of Dancing.

She feels soft, surprisingly small.
Her chin tucks against my chest.
I breathe in the fragrance of orchids
or Mary.

The song ends,
we stand still.
Mary keeps her hand in mine.
We stand like statues of people dancing,
waiting for the dance to begin.

I'm fourteen. It's August and our bags are packed for vacation. Even in Springfield, the time has come to start locking doors.

Ticket Money

Talk about creepy, finding out you've been robbed,
I guess the guy just walks in.
The door isn't locked — our fault.
He walks in, broad daylight, like he lives here,
goes upstairs, helps himself to the suitcases on the beds.
Takes the money in my metal box —
everything I earned all summer mowing yards.

Walks out with our suitcases full of clothes
like it's his vacation instead of ours.
Well, it is now.

Police figure he's on drugs,
coming in here at 10 AM,
rummaging through our things.
Lucky, they say, we weren't home.
He buys a ticket with small bills
on a Greyhound bus for Joplin,
slips off along the way and disappears.

You know now he won't get caught.
He gets away with being here,
walking around, touching our things,
taking what he wants.
My room feels dirty.

I'm fourteen. *In class pictures I'm always in the back row with the tallest kids. My appetite is amazing, but all that food just makes me taller.*

Anatomy Lesson

Some guys' biceps stretch their shirtsleeves.
My arms dangle like limp white rope.
Maybe they're thicker than they look.
I hope.

Muscles bulge on some guys' chests.
Mine is mostly skin and bones,
ribs poked out like Thanksgiving
turkey breast.

My only chance is to fill out later.
Just once I want a pretty girl
to glance at me and see
a gladiator.

I'm fourteen. *When we're little, we take for granted that our family and friends will always be there with us. Later on we find out differently.*

Watching Geese

Geese fly over.
I think of him
honking silly like a goose.
The geese never landed
but we didn't care.
Who needs
a friend like that?

Who needs a guy
who cracks you up
with jokes you never tell your mom,
and you wonder where
he gets such stupid stuff?

The halls at school
are full of kids,
but no one looks for me.

No one tells me like it is,
borrows shirts that disappear,
knows our house as well as his.

Now he's gone and won't be back.

I'm watching geese, thinking of him.
Do I miss his funny grin?
Who needs a friend like that?

I'm fifteen. Mr. Moffatt is a serious trombone teacher. He's serious about everything. I'm his best student and I'm serious, too. But one day another side of me slips out.

The Lesson

My trombone teacher stands beside me,
listens intently, touches his lips,
lifts his chin
as I go for high C.

I've washed my horn.
The shiny bell is a golden mirror
of his expressions.

He nods, presses his lips together,
arches his eyebrows unaware
his reflection makes me think
chimpanzee.

Unexpectedly I laugh.
Without warning, notes splatter,
blast from the bell.

I stop, apologize, explain.
His smile thin, we carry on.

But there he is again in the bell,
my last thread of control gone.

It gets worse
until at last, his patience worn,
he stops the lesson.

Too embarrassed to say more,
I pack my horn,
leap down the steps two at a time
stifling guilty pleasure.

I'm fifteen. My collections now fill one room in our house. The years of field trips and chance discoveries are adding up.

The Naturalist

A guy with a net never knows
where the next butterfly might lead him.
I've sloshed up creeks,
leaped ditches,
sneezed my way through goldenrod,
ambushed fritillaries in the woods.

Once, chasing a swallowtail,
halfway across a hilly field
I met a bull.

Picture this:
swallowtail soaring higher,
boy running for his life,
grim bull gathering speed.

The swallowtail made it over the fence
with me flying behind.
All I got that day was a funny story.

Being a collector, either way
life is never dull.
Everything I catch, or don't,
becomes another story
of me, my net, nature,
and the occasional bull.

I'm fifteen. My *first official job is working mornings in a grocery store.*
Cleaning up after the store's bakers is not what I expected. I last a week.

Kryptonite Blues

I'm elbow-deep in soapy water.
Hands?
Boiling — medium rare.
Glasses fogged,
uniform sweaty-wet through.

What do bakers do in here?

Batter dries like kryptonite.

Scalding water turns egg-goo
to sap.

How can sugar stick to walls?
I hope that stain
is cherry juice.
Who spills flour on the floor
and skates through it?

No!
What are those things?
Must have been a thousand mice!
I'll never eat another raisin roll.

Cleaning after bakers
is a dirty stinking job!
Mom's no help.
She just grins,
"Welcome to my world."

I'm fifteen. My parents want to adopt a child. I think it will be great. Especially after I meet the baby.

Meeting Jule

Mom holds the baby,
we listen to agency talk.
Dad's quiet.

Mom hands him the little girl.
I've never seen him hold a baby,
didn't know he knew how.
After a while it's my turn.

She's so small!
Pretty little dimpled hands,
miniature fingers hold my own,
eyes blue as a porcelain doll's
blink at me.

She stretches,
yawns with her whole face,
tiny lids slide shut
like delicate window shades.

Talk goes on, but what's to say?
She's picked out her big brother,
I hold my sleepy sister in my arms.

I'm fifteen. *In March I'll take my driver's test. Learning to drive,*
I'm discovering, calls for someone you can trust.

* *

Conspirators

I brake to a stop, check the mirror,
maneuver the gearshift into reverse.
"Good job," Mom says, sitting beside me.
"Your dad will be surprised!"

I grin, remembering other times
she's said the same —

> *backyard forts*
> *she helped me build and furnish . . .*

We creep down the alley in reverse,
this time making it all the way.

> *coffee grounds in corncob pipes,*
> *us too silly to breathe . . .*

The gears grind loudly,
we wince and laugh,

> *the first biscuits I baked from scratch*
> *"almost" by myself . . .*

I get it in low, lurch forward, glad she's there.
At times like this you need someone
with a sense of humor.

I'm fifteen. Flirting can't be as hard as I'm making it. It seems to come naturally to some guys.

I Think I Need a Manual

Some guys flirt with all the girls.
Doesn't work for me, I've tried.

> *Knock-knock.*
>
> Who's there?
>
> *Ima.*
>
> Ima who?
>
> *Ima guess
> I'm too tongue-tied.*

Every time I try to flirt
I feel my face begin to burn.

> *Knock-knock.*
>
> Who's there?
>
> *Wanda.*
>
> Wanda who?
>
> *Wanda when
> I'll ever learn.*

I need to think of something clever,
all I do is blather on.

> *Knock-knock.*
>
> Who's there?
>
> *Doris.*
>
> Doris who?
>
> *Doris open,
> squirrel's gone.*

The secret is to loosen up,
but flirting makes me so uptight.

> *Knock-knock.*
>
> Who's there?
>
> *Wilma.*
>
> Wilma who?
>
> *Wilma ever
> get it right?*

I'm fifteen. *Some things never change, our fascination with teachers, for example. When I was little, I thought teachers lived at school.*

Grapevine

When Miss B. wears the red blouse,
we think up reasons to stand by her desk.

If Mrs. M. smiled, her face would crack,
but every Saturday afternoon
she takes her parents riding.
How can a teacher that old have parents?

I don't know if it's true or not,
but rumor says Miss B. will take a drink.

Mr. J. is getting divorced.
They say it's nasty.
Mr. A. paints houses during the summer.

One year for Christmas
two older students
bought Miss B. a bottle.
She didn't give it back, either,
so they say.

When I was little, I saw my teacher buying shoes.
I talked about it constantly for a week.
I wonder why we talk so much about our teachers.

Take Miss B.
All I know is she's not married.
If she wants to have a private life,
who would know?

I'm fifteen. Some of my friends are driving now. Driving brings new freedom, sometimes at a price.

· ·

The News

"Have you heard about Abby?"

You know what's coming
is going to be bad —
but not horrible,
not in a car,
coming home from a party.
The news is hard as twisted steel.

"Have you heard about Abby?"

Not wanting to say the words,
we keep passing her name around.
The news flashes down the hall
like a receding car.

"Have you heard about Abby?"

"Have you heard about Abby?"

I'm sixteen. That smart blonde in Spanish class finally speaks to me. It's a start!

. . . .

Puppy Love

"Buy a ticket?"

Golden hair,
fabulous freckles,
green eyes
crinkling at me.

I stall for time.
Who wouldn't?
"What do I win?"

She hands me a picture.
"The cutest puppy
you ever saw.
Look at its floppy ears."

Those green eyes.
I flirt back,
        stretching it out.
"Promise I'll win?"

"How can you lose?"

I hand back the picture,
reach for my pocket.
"I'll take a chance."

I'm sixteen. Being a pitcher is great when you win. When you lose, you find out who your friends are.

Teammates

Game's over.
I slump on the bench,
stare at my glove.

The guys are down, too,
but they pat my shoulder.
"Shake it off."

I don't look up.
What can I say?
I just walked in
the winning run.

I reach down,
pull off my cleats.

They pat my shoulder
anyway.

"Shake it off," they say.

I'm sixteen. Long arms come in handy after all. I used to be skinny, now I'm a pitcher.

Looking for Strike Three

My first no-hitter down to this —
one last fastball
faster than the batter.
My shoulder burns.

George squats,
pulls down his mask,
flashes the sign,
all eyes on me.

I start the rock, pump, kick,
the baseball catapults toward home.
The batter's swing is level, quick.

The ball pops into friendly leather.
Guys rush to pound my back.
When you win like this,
it doesn't get much better.

I'm seventeen. *One more year of high school. A few more trips to play in orchestra concerts. A few more lessons to learn.*

When Words Fail

Some sounds stop me
whatever I'm doing:
mosquito-hum around my head, suddenly silent,
crows cawing down a river . . .

Here's another —
the last sound you'd expect
to make a list.
At All-State Orchestra we rehearse
a piece that features an oboist.

She sits as if alone and plays
the way I bet she does each day,
working to make the notes her own,
teaching her oboe what it can do.

What flows out that tiny bell
is not your typical reedy whine,
but notes so sweet that
one by one
we sit —
like in church —
to listen.

Honey dripping off the comb.
Water trickling over stone.
Bird choruses at dawn.

I know these words are not the best.
We have to hear for ourselves, I guess,
pure sounds like excellence.

I'm nineteen. The nation is electing a president. For the first time, I've paid attention to the talk. I've decided to vote.

The Volunteer

"First time?"
I nod, a little uncertain.
The volunteer smiles,
checks my registration.
"Good for you, young man!" he says.

He shows me where to sign,
shakes my hand, pats it,
hands me a ballot.
"Gotta make your voice heard!"

I mark my choices,
drop the ballot into the box,
smiling.
"See you next time!" the volunteer says.

I came in feeling
like a kid at his parents' party.
Now I'm a voter.

I walk out waving
to the guy who helped me.
If he ran for office,
I'd vote for him.

Section Three
Over 20

In Your
Wildest Dreams

Some of the experiences you'll find in the next poems happened in the past for me but may lie in the future for you. Do you ever wonder how it feels to leave home and be on your own? Get married? Have children? I have grandchildren. Can you, in your wildest dreams, imagine having grandchildren? Maybe not. But when the time comes, you'll love them. I promise.

One thing we all understand is love. I've been blessed with a lot of that. "Night Songs" is about my wife and me. It's my favorite poem in the book.

I'm twenty-two. At Drury College I major in biology. My senior year I take a creative writing class. My professor gives me advice I don't expect.

Revising

Dr. Graham says keep it up
I'll be a writer.
Me, a writer?
No way!

Wouldn't that be something?
I slip out my story,
remembering nights I couldn't stop
searching for words to say it right,
celebrating small victories.

I flip through the pages,
reading his notes.
Too late, right?
Too many other things to do.
Too many plans.

Wouldn't that be something?
Without knowing I've crossed the line,
in my mind I'm a writer.

I'm twenty-two. Sandy and I have been dating for six years, ever since I bought that raffle ticket. I wound up with something far better than a puppy.

. . . .

Getting It Right

Last night we practiced
how she'd walk
down the aisle
on her father's arm.
We practiced
where we'd stand,
what we'd say.

But today
her wedding gown makes it real.
Standing together,
holding hands,
saying I do —
from this day forward,
we're real.

I'm twenty-two. We just got married. We're headed to Atlanta where I'll attend graduate school at Emory University. This goodbye is different.

Goodbyes

All of a sudden
I'm leaving home.
I've never gone away before,
not like this,
not as a husband,
not for good.

I'll see them at Christmas,
Easter maybe,
next spring.

All of a sudden
I'm out of time,
no time to think,
talk,
tell them how I feel
about this long-awaited
scary grand moment.

I'll write them a letter,
call,
we'll talk.

All of a sudden
I'm gone.

I'm twenty-three. Sandy is having our first baby. I feel useless. I think she agrees.

Waiting for Robin

Eyes wide
my wife stares at the ceiling.

"You all right?"
Dumb thing to say,
of course she's not.
What can I do?

She grabs my hand
with startling strength,
hair plastered, face wet.

I squeeze back.
She looks at me
from somewhere else.

Becoming a mother
is all there
in my wife's eyes.

Song of the Swing Set

The three-headed creature
huddles together in the yard.

In the space between the big head
and the instructions on the grass,
the helper heads bob in and out.

The three-headed creature sings to itself
two simple songs at once.

When are we going to get to swing?
      Stop playing with the screwdriver.
When are we going to get to swing?
      Where did you drop the washers?
When are we going to get to swing?
      Let's look for Section C.
When are we going to get to swing?
      Why don't you play with Mommy?

I'm thirty-two. Having a family is a serious responsibility. But being grown up doesn't mean we have to turn in our Peter Pan passes.

A Matter of Timing

I'll tell you what's silly —
sitting there holding
a *National Geographic*
with pictures of St. John Island.
(That's not the silly part.)

"It's the prettiest place
I've ever seen.
Do you think we could ever
afford to go?"
(Get the picture?)

"Let's do it now,
a once-in-a-lifetime
dream vacation."
(It's coming.)

So here we are
in the prettiest place
we've ever seen,
our footprints
close together in the sand.
I squeeze her hand,
she smiles back.

We're married with kids,
for Pete's sake,
with a mortgage to pay.
Utterly irresponsible.
Aren't we silly?

Little Gray Wolf

Begs to move
A little faster —
"We'll be late.
It isn't fair."

Can't believe
It takes so long —
"Dad, we'll be
The last ones there."

War-whoops off
To catch the rest
While I unpack
In the August sun.

Across the field,
Along the stream,
He runs with braves
Intent on fun.

Hours later,
Daylight fading,
Flops beside me,
"When do we eat?"

Wolfing hot dogs
Under stars,
Yawning, nodding
At my feet.

Not too big
To lift and carry,
Not too old
To hug him tight.

Little Gray Wolf,
Rambunctious boy,
Snoring brave,
My joy. Goodnight.

I'm thirty-seven. *For the past three years our son Jeff and I have traveled fifty miles to camp on Beaver Creek in southwest Missouri. It's a guys-only thing. Big sister Robin objects to our policy.*

The Co-Ed Issue at Camp Little Hatchet

Camp Little Hatchet —
manly odors of tent and hot dogs,
potatoes burnt to blackened shells
in a rock-circle guy-fire.

Last bastion of rugged males
hidden in weeds that would make girls cry
about snakes and spiders lurking nearby.

Butterfly nets and water skis
leaning ready against trees,
boat pulled up by masculine muscles
onto the bank.

"What do you think?"
We're getting ready to slap steaks
thick and juicy the way guys like them
onto the grill.
"Invite the girls for the last night?"

"Never allowed girls before.
 Think they'd come?"

"Don't care if they do,
don't care if they don't."

"I guess we could call."

Our guests arrive in time to eat.
They don't make fun,
and that's important.
We're glad to see them, even here.
We let them stay.

I'm forty. Sometimes I think back to when I was a boy. When I was three, my parents kept a turtle in the basement. I used to slide the poor thing around like a hockey puck. Now I'm sorry.

Daydreams

I remember the turtle
beneath our basement stair.
I see him sleeping there.

Maybe he's dreaming of clover,
shade beside a tree,
days when he was free.

When he awakes he lurches,
searches through the gloom
around across the room,
scratches at the stones.
Methodically he crawls,
scrapes against the walls.

The walls mark his prison,
but even if he knows,
on and on he goes.

I remember the turtle —
when I was only three —
whose courage was lost on me.

I'm forty-five. I loved camping at Whitehorse Lake in Arizona, even with occasional bear scares. I caught my first fish in that lake.

Things We Prize

Hidden in the mountains, fed by snow,
The lake was small. We stayed there every year
And got to know our neighbors camping near
In tents like toadstools growing in a row.

I found a secret pool, a little nook
Where I could lie and watch the fish below.
But no amount of coaxing made them go
For worms or bits of bacon on my hook.

At last a fish too hungry to be wise
Took my bait so hard its body shook.
"A fish!" I cried. "Big enough to cook!"
I held it high to show its mighty size.

Even though the lake is far away,
I remember posing with my prize
And grinning at our neighbors' happy cries
Just as though it happened yesterday.

I've caught some bigger fish but this is clear:
They'll never match the thrill I felt that day.
No matter what those larger trophies weigh
The first fish will always be most dear.

I'm forty-eight. Sandy and I are "empty-nesters," as they say. Our kids are gone. We can do what we want, go where we choose. It's just the two of us, more or less.

· ·

Travel Companions

Riding a bus in Denali Park, Alaska,
somewhere near the highest pass,
with mountains poking through the clouds
and valleys deep in mist below,
our guide spots an eagle nest
down along a canyon wall.

Perched there on the edge of space —
a young eagle!
Amazing sight.
Magnificent youngster sitting alone,
weighing the world from the edge of home.

I think to myself, he's not quite ready,
he's getting the nerve to test his wings.
It won't be long before he'll fly.
Before you know it, he'll be gone.

Suddenly he's Robin and Jeff,
who grew fast as young eagles do,
weighed the world from their own nest
until they were ready.

Then they flew.

I'm fifty. Our daughter Robin is getting married. It's a time for joy. But other emotions can ambush you.

Shower Thoughts

Watching Robin open gifts,
I hear her laughter
from a distance.

I'm thinking ahead.
I know they'll ask,
"Who gives this bride?"

I'll answer properly of course.
It's a small part,
a traditional thing.
All I do is say,
"Her mother and I."

But even now I know
how hard that will be.
Times like this,
mothers show their real strength.
Sandy smiles,
scoops up wrappings,
pours coffee, serves dessert.

I sit in a corner,
dreading the words.

I'm fifty-three. In another year I'll publish my first book of humorous poetry about school. I'm working outside at our patio table when I have an unexpected visitor.

Today's Poem

On a sunny day I sit outside
scribbling away at a poem,
something I hope will be funny,
when he creeps around the side of my house,
tiny nose searching the air
for the only smell he recognizes.
Baby opossum doesn't know
he's standing on my shoe.

Sitting still, I look down
like some Greek god on high,
see the little fellow's plight,
know (or guess) that what he seeks
is growing cold beyond his reach.

I understand his tragedy,
grieve that soon his life must end.
I know, too, today's poem
will be for him.

I'm sixty-two. When I was twelve, Billy Pauly and I found a skull in a cave. We kept the skull as a trophy. Now I'm not sure we did the right thing.

Guilt

1949

We found it buried in a cave
coated with clay
dark as blood.
"Human skull," Billy whispered.
"Probably a murder!"

His father smiled,
turned the skull
casually as a football.
"What you found," he chuckled,
"is a bear."

1999

With great care
the paleontologist studies the skull.
"Where did you find it?"
he wants to know.
"This bear lived
ten thousand years ago."

Ten thousand years.
Ten thousand years
this skull rested
pillowed on clay,
safe in its black cave coffin —
until that day.

He hands it back.
I don't know what to say.

I'm sixty-two. *I'm a grandfather now. Robin is married with two boys of her own. I tease them the same way I used to tease her, the same way my father teased me.*

When Kristopher and Tyler Come Calling

I open the door
And pretend to ignore
Them standing there.

"Where'd they go?"
(They know I know.)
"This isn't fair."

I heave a sigh
And dry my eye.
"Is that their car?"

With a puzzled frown
I look down,
And there they are!

Grins and giggles,
Hugs and wiggles.
"Joke's on me!"

It's a corny game,
Always the same,
And the love comes free.

I'm sixty-five. Sandy and I have been married forty-three years. My dad used to call us bookends because we went together so well. We still smile about that.

Night Songs

As starry hours slowly sweep
We turn together in our sleep.
Sometimes I wake and watch her there
In rumpled sheets and tangled hair
Pillow tucked beneath her head
Breathing near me on the bed —
A quiet every-night event —
Then drift away again, content.

Outside in dimly shadowed light
Voices thrum away the night
And as they sing their ancient themes
We mingle in each other's dreams.
Time moves softly, slow and deep,
We turn together in our sleep
Until the morning comes and then
She wakes and life begins again.